The intent and purpose of this volume is to give you faith, hope and inspiration. Hopefully it will help bring peace and tranquility into your life. May it be a reminder of God's love, guidance and His many blessings.

Our publications help to support our work for needy children in over 120 countries around the world. Through our programs, thousands of children are fed, clothed, educated, sheltered and given the opportunity to live decent lives.

Salesian Missions wishes to extend special thanks and gratitude to our generous poet friends and to the publishers who have given us permission to reprint material included in this book. Every effort has been made to give proper acknowledgments. Any omissions or errors are deeply regretted, and the publisher, upon notification, will be pleased to make the necessary corrections in subsequent editions.

Copyright © 2000 by Salesian Missions, 2 Lefevre Lane, New Rochelle, New York 10801-5710. All Rights Reserved. © 46270

First Edition Printed in the U.S.A. by Concord Litho Group, Inc., Concord, New Hampshire 03301.

Splendor and Majesty

from the Salesian Collection

Compiled and edited by
Jennifer Grimaldi

Illustrated by
Russell Bushée, Frank Massa,
Paul Scully, Dorian Lee Remine,
Maureen McCarthy, Helen M.L. Kunic,
Gail Pepin, Jessica Wheeler,
and Robert Van Steinburg

Contents

Friendship 7	I Thank Thee, Lord 38
The Ladder of Success 8	A Morning Prayer 40
Tomorrow 10	A Few of My Favorite Things 41
Spring's Entrance 11	Learn to Wait 42
The Measure of a Man 12	With His Love 44
A Friend 14	Rise and Look Ahead 45
A Small Boy's World 15	The Changing of the Guard .. 46
Ship of Dreams 17	Enter Autumn 48
God Loves Me So 18	Autumn Really Shines 49
Summertime 19	Autumn in My Heart 50
Little White Church 21	Autumn Is a Gypsy Season 52
Dare to Dream 22	Autumn's Aria 53
What Autumn Shares 23	Hold Fast to Your Mem'ries .. 54
A Secret Place 24	Guiding Faith 56
God Created Happiness 26	God Guides My Path 57
The Gift of Friendship 27	May God's Love Abide
One More Day 28	Within You 58
A Picture of Peace 30	Prayer Power 60
Velvet Slippers 31	Blessed Friend 61
A Gift of God's Glory 32	Beauty and Splendor 63
Promises of Spring 34	It's Spring Again! 64
My Friend 35	In Silence 65
Without a Doubt 36	Home 66
The Creative Hand of God 37	Summer's Umbrella 68

Butterflies	69
A Greater God	70
As God Gives	72
More Than the Sun	73
Aftermath	74
God Has Shown the Way	76
Summer Glory	77
Sermon on the Shore	79
Troubled Waters	80
Peace, Be Still	81
Autumn Magic	82
Interlude	84
I Lose My Heart to Autumn	85
The Right Road	86
Nature's Tapestries	88
Where Did the Summer Go?	89
Winter's Silence	90
Winter's Snow	92
Winter's Magic	93
Climb Your Mountain	94
Memories	96
There Is Time	97
Springtime's Grand Design	98
Springtime	99
Together	100
Early Spring	102
Renewal	103
Safe in His Arms	104
Summertime Sunday	106
Farewell, Green Fields	107
Life's Road	108
Winds	110
Knee-Deep in Beauty	111
The Narrow Path	112
September Days	114
Autumn Winds	115
Old Country Church Beside the Road	116
I Love My Little Home, Dear Lord	118
God Gives the Full-Ear Yield	119
An Autumntime Melody	120
Winter Jewel	122
Come Winter	123
Earth's Dark Floor and Snowflakes	124
Treasure Beneath the Snow	126
A Little Country Church	128

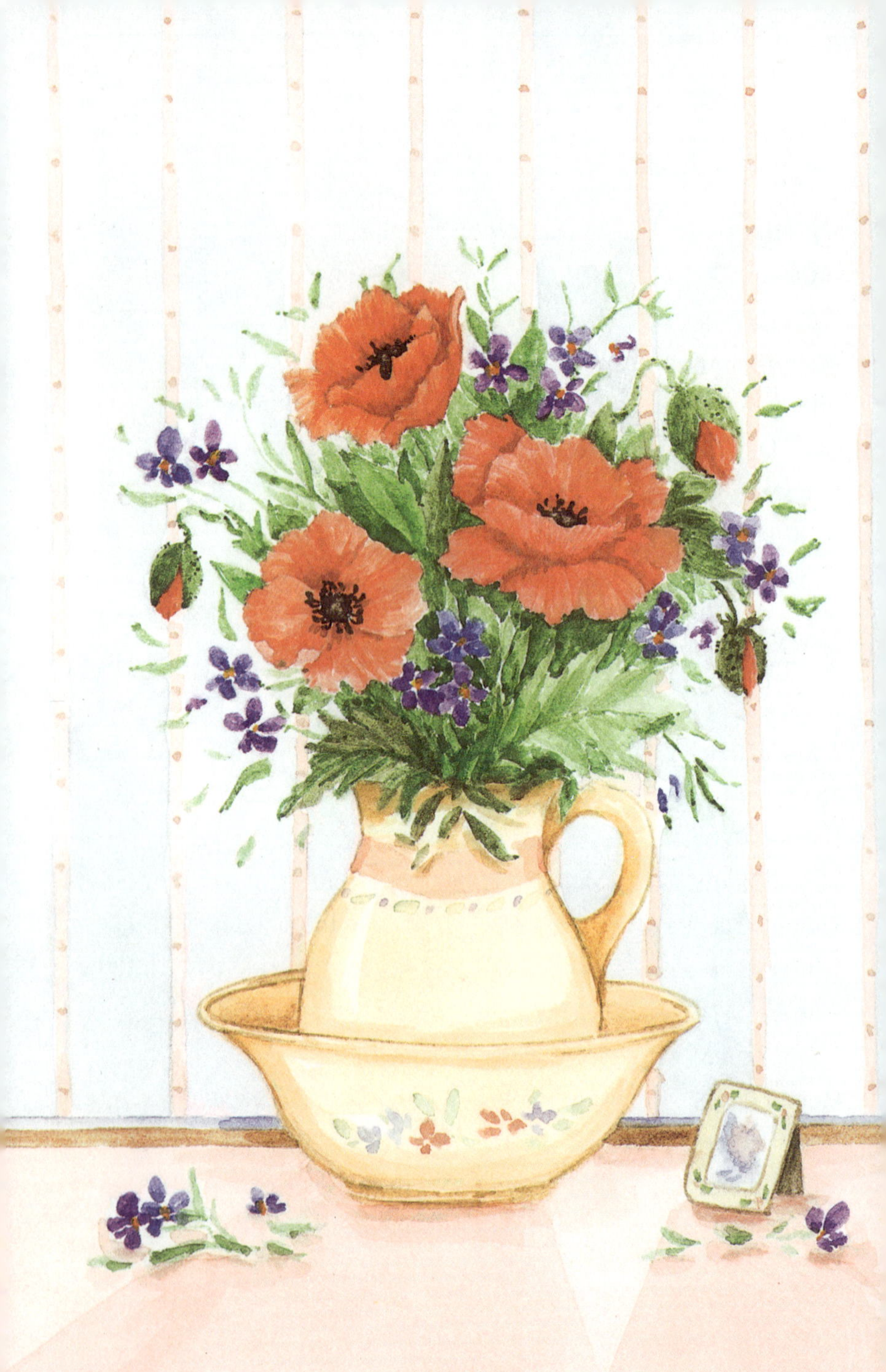

Friendship...

It's like a rosebud in a vase,
A sunset in the sky,
The sound of laughter from a child
And the taste of lemon pie...

It's like a rosebud in a vase,
A light and gentle breeze,
The feel of velvet, soft and warm,
And the scent of mellow cheese...

It's like a rosebud in a vase,
A bright and cheerful hue,
The look of Autumn in the trees
And the gift of knowing you!

Hope C. Oberhelman

*A faithful friend is a sturdy shelter;
he who finds one finds a treasure.*
Sirach 6:14

The Ladder of Success

We like to think that we have climbed
The ladder of success.
Rung by rung, we laud ourselves
While seeking happiness.

Too often we forget to thank
The One who makes us great –
The Lord of lords, and King of kings,
Whose mercy seals our fate.

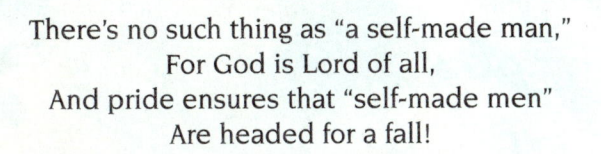

There's no such thing as "a self-made man,"
For God is Lord of all,
And pride ensures that "self-made men"
Are headed for a fall!

It's what we do in Jesus' name
That brings us happiness.
It's what we do to honor Him
That measures our success.

In the precious name of Jesus,
We climb to lofty heights
And there we find true happiness
And spiritual delights.

Clay Harrison

Tomorrow

Tomorrow will be soon enough –
So many of us say,
But why put off until tomorrow
What we can do today?

We could give so much more help
To those who are in need;
Put words of Jesus in their hearts
That unsaved souls be freed.

Yes, we know we should be doing this
And tomorrow we will start.
Oh no, my friend, the time is now;
Dear Lord, please touch our hearts.

Tomorrows seldom ever come
When we put them off today;
Let's ask the Lord to give us strength
To do tomorrows right away.

Albert Theel

Spring's Entrance

Spring at last unlocks the door
And thrusts it open wide,
And like a fairy with a wand,
Bedecks the countryside.

First, she brings the softest rain
To moisten all the earth,
And then instructs the tiny seeds
To grow for all they're worth.

Each day, new beauty comes in view;
The buds take shape and form,
And blossoming has now begun
From soil, so soft and warm.

Once more our hearts rejoice to see
The miracle of Spring;
High up somewhere in a tree,
We hear a robin sing!

The greening hills and leafy trees
All cast a magic spell.
When God, in nature, does His work,
We know that all is well.

Gene Appleby

*Enter, let us bow down in
worship; let us kneel before
the Lord who made us.*
Psalm 95:6

The Measure of a Man

Most people measure age in years,
There must be other ways
To count our time upon this earth
And to record our days.
What makes so many shy away
From all that's less than young?
When only in our latter years,
Our sweetest songs are sung.

We who now must walk with care
Are those who used to run,
But aged hearts hold memories
Of laughter and of fun.

God never meant for man to be
Forever young and strong;
We lose some things and some we save
As we move right along.

For each of us God has a plan
That's not confined to years,
And everyone's allotted
His share of smiles and tears.
Whatever age we are we must
Become the best we can,
For imitating Christ becomes
…The measure of a man.

Grace E. Easley

*Great is our Lord, vast in power,
with wisdom beyond measure.*
Psalm 147:5

A Friend

Just when the night seems darkest
And the world is closing in,
You sense a ray of sunshine
In the presence of a friend.

A friend who quickly lifts you
From the depths of hurt and pain
And soon puts back a smile
Upon your face again.

A true friend is your anchor
Who helps keep your boat afloat.
Despite all the stormy weather,
Your friend is your pillar of hope.

When you have a true, true friend,
You surely have been blessed.
To know they are there, regardless,
Helps make your life its best.

Gloria Swan Kennedy

A Small Boy's World

A little boy with laughing eyes
Looked up into the April skies,
Then gently did the blue skies weep –
A raindrop kissed his chubby cheek,
One tender moment, bright with fun,
Then once again the springtime sun.

A little boy with joys untold
Found magic in the sun of gold.
His heart delighted happily
In playfulness, so bright and free.
Somehow he captured Nature fair
And tossed aside each worldly care.

It takes so little, it would seem,
To satisfy a small boy's dream;
He finds it all from day to day
Within the hours of happy play.
A million miracles unfurled…
The magic in a small boy's world.

Garnett Ann Schultz

Guide me in Your truth and teach me, for You are God my Savior. For You I wait all the long day, because of Your goodness, Lord.
Psalm 25:5

Ship of Dreams

Build me a ship – my goddess of dreams –
Make me the captain and crew;
Pour me an ocean to play on the shores
Where dreams are fulfilling and new.

Set me to sail – by light of the moon –
Give me one star for a guide;
Will me the strength to stand at the wheel
And challenge the tempest and tide.

All of my dreams are shattered and torn;
All of my hopes are forlorn.
Build me a ship to take me away
To the island where dreams are born.

                Michael Dubina

God Loves Me So

There are snares along life's pathway,
Hidden dangers do abound;
But with briars I see roses
Springing up from stony ground.

Though at times I walk through darkness,
Still I feel God's presence near.
With each dawning rises hope,
Canceling my doubt and fear.

Many are the disappointments;
Who counts all the tears which flow?
Yet, in sorrow I find solace
When I think God loves me so.

Regina Wiencek

Summertime

As I was looking from my window
On a lovely Summer day,
God just seemed to speak to me
In a warm and special way.

It seemed that He was saying,
"It's time to let you know.
I love you all so very much
I just had to let it show."

The trees were standing straight and tall,
Their branches reaching high.
The birds were flying in the air
And looking toward the sky.

With flowers blooming everywhere
And tall, green grass to mow,
The sky was filled with clouds above,
The sun just seemed to glow.

The beauty was so splendid,
I just had to stop and say,
"I thank You, God, so very much
For this great Summer day."

Bonnie Knapp

But I can enter Your house because of Your great love. I can worship in Your holy temple because of my reverence for You, Lord.
Psalm 5:8

Little White Church

There's a little white church in the valley
Where the bells ring out loud and clear,
Calling all the people to worship,
Coming there from far and near.

In this little white church in the valley,
The people all come to pray,
And the hymns they sing will float out gently
And echo all along the way.

In this little white church in the valley,
They will open up their hearts in love
And give thanks for all of their blessings
Bestowed on them by God up above.

In the little white church in the valley,
They'll be welcomed whether rich or poor,
And together they will face their transgressions
And there'll be peace in the valley evermore.

        Mary Ellen Porter Dole

Dare to Dream

Dare to dream when days are at their darkest,
When stones of heartache barricade the road.
Look up beyond the stars and past the shadows,
Span the spheres and lighten half your load.
Count not the weary miles you leave behind you,
But add the joys you find along the way.
Beyond compare the shining hope awakened,
Within the words "somewhere," "somehow," "someway."
Shed the shell that houses dormant courage,
Build decision's tower strong and high,
Turn your back upon the lesser moments,
Spread your wings, for your were meant to fly!
Anyone can wade a narrow stream,
To swim an ocean you must dare to dream!

Grace E. Easley

What Autumn Shares

We are sure that none compares
To the wonders Autumn shares,
Colors bright of every hue
Nestled 'neath a sky of blue,
Golden moments – clouds of white,
Autumn smiles in sweet delight.

Summer bids a fond farewell,
Captured in September's spell.
Harvest trees are bending low
Just before the cold and snow,
Solemn woods with leaves piled deep,
Mother Nature rests in sleep.

Summer birds have flown away,
Waiting for a springtime day.
Melancholy time of year,
Winter lingers very near.
We bid farewell to Summer's cares
And thrill to joys the Autumn shares.

Garnett Ann Schultz

*Then the Lord looked upon the earth,
and filled it with His blessings.*
Sirach 16:27

A Secret Place

Each of us needs a secret spot,
A place where we can go
To meditate or reminisce
As memories merge and grow…

Into the times we've loved the most
Or the image, perhaps, of a friend.
In quiet nooks we can weave our dreams
For past times never end.

Unless we find such a special place
Far away from humdrum cares,
We walk along a lonely path
Where sometimes no one shares…

Our intimate thoughts, so deeply felt,
That age cannot erase.
Oh, thank You, God, for giving us
A secret, private place…

A well-marked spot where we can go
Whatever it be our choice.
Life is not complete unless we hear
Your soothing, helpful voice.

Jean Conder Soule

Know that the Lord works wonders for the faithful; the Lord hears when I call out.
Psalm 4:4

God Created Happiness

God created happiness
'Cause it makes a spirit soar,
And if you're feeling joyous,
It's a gift from Heaven's store.
Neither wealth nor fame can buy it,
For happiness must bubble up within
And overflow to others
'Til another soul it wins.
When you meet someone who's happy
And he's whistling a pleasant tune,
You'll, too, feel more chipper
If you join in very soon.
You need not search for happiness,
For it dwells within the heart and soul,
Just give a bit more of yourself
And before you know it you'll be full!
For God created happiness
And formed each smiling face,
Just trust His grace and goodness
And each "frown" He will erase!

Linda C. Grazulis

The Gift of Friendship

Friendship is a priceless gift
That cannot be bought or sold,
But its value is far greater
Than a mountain of gold –
For gold is cold and lifeless,
It can neither see nor hear,
And in the time of trouble
It is powerless to cheer,
It has no ears to listen,
No heart to understand,
It cannot bring you comfort,
Or reach out a helping hand,
So when you ask God for a gift,
Be thankful if He sends,
Not diamonds, pearls or riches,
But the love of real true friends.

Helen Steiner Rice

Used with permission of
The Helen Steiner Rice Foundation
Suite 2100, Atrium Two
221 East Fourth Street
Cincinnati, OH 45202

One More Day

I see some snowflakes swirling around,
Floating gently to the ground.
Each and every one I see
Is completely different, like you and me.

Beautifully molded by God's own hand,
I watch them as they gently land.
These wonderful things He did create,
Soon will bow to time and fate.

These snow-white droplets from the sky
Sadly remind me of you and I –
We each have moments on earth to spend,
Not knowing when our time will end.

One common bond we have to share,
'Twas God's own hands that put us there,
Whatever time on earth we've spent
Was a wondrous blessing, Heaven sent.

God bestows to all on earth
Priceless moments beyond worth,
To Him we humbly kneel and pray
That He might grant us one more day.

Joseph Ferrara

A Picture of Peace

I wake to a beautiful morning…
What a wonderful sight I see –
The earth's turned white overnight.
What a picture He painted for me!

Gone is the heat of Summer,
Gone is each sultry day,
Gone are the dried and fallen leaves
The winds have whisked away.

All is buried beneath the snow,
Bushes and shrubs disappear.
Chimneys belch smoke from rooftops high,
Icicles hang, crystal clear.

A look of joy and contentment
Lies over the land that I see.
And so this delightful picture
Brings peace to the heart of me.

Angie Monnens

Velvet Slippers

Like velvet slippers, snow dances in,
   Quietly throughout the night;
   And on the wings of morning,
   The sun awakes to shed its light.

We delight to see the glistening snow,
   Sparkling, as it creates a scene.
   It blankets a gray and frozen world
   With lacy crystals, fresh and clean.

Soon the velvet slippers prance no more,
   For like a song, the dance must end.
   But only for a little while –
   When once again, snow dances in.

   Barbara Cagle Ray

A Gift of God's Glory

I can see in the heavens
A moonlight of love;
It's a gift of God's glory
Sent down from above.

All the starshine above me
Looks so pretty in space,
There's a cloud dressed in cotton
And it seems to have a face.

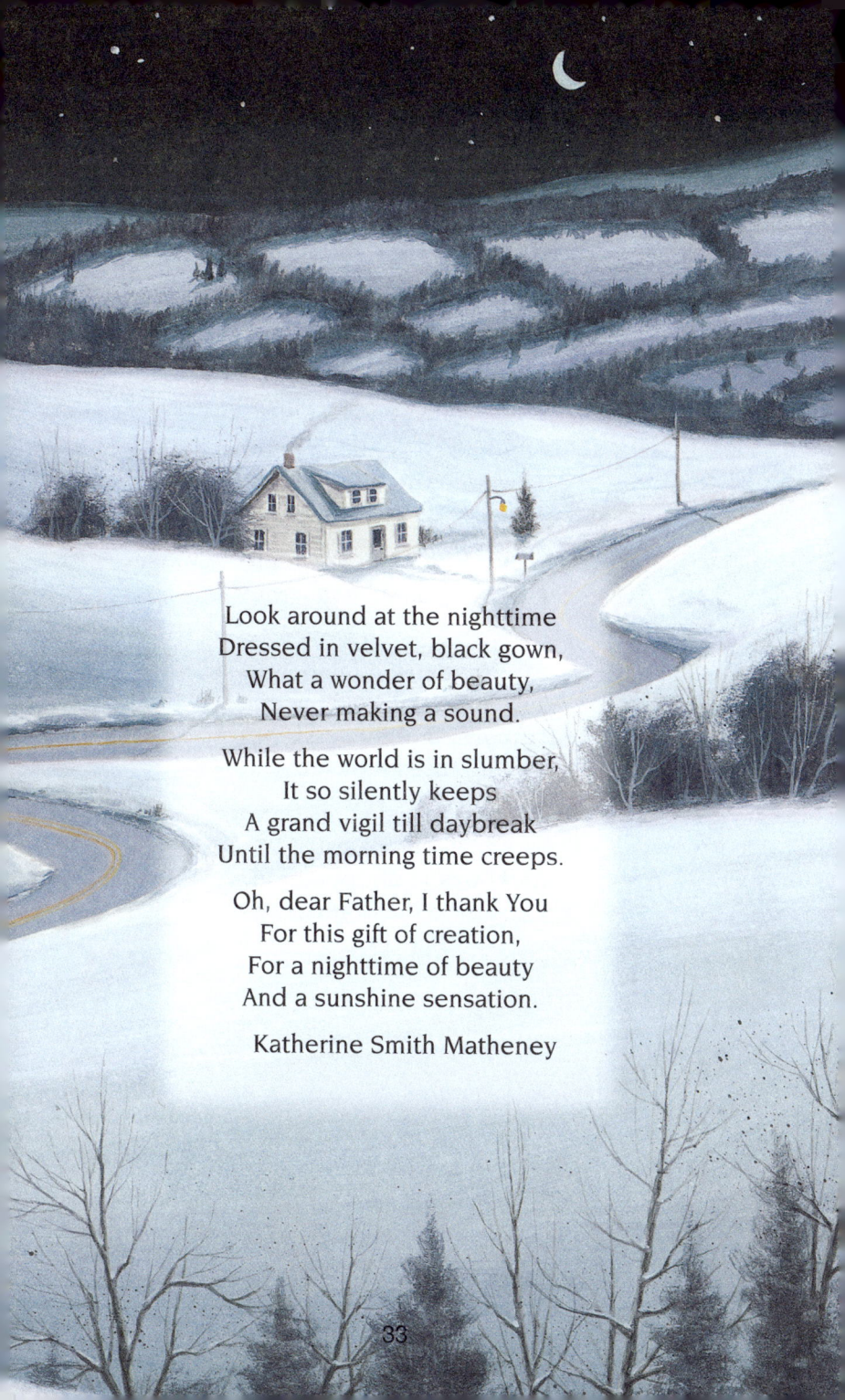

Look around at the nighttime
Dressed in velvet, black gown,
What a wonder of beauty,
Never making a sound.

While the world is in slumber,
It so silently keeps
A grand vigil till daybreak
Until the morning time creeps.

Oh, dear Father, I thank You
For this gift of creation,
For a nighttime of beauty
And a sunshine sensation.

Katherine Smith Matheney

Promises of Spring

April promised lilacs
And tulip gifts of gold.
She promised gentle raindrops
And wildflowers colored bold.

April promised pathways
Strewn with emerald green.
She promised panoramic views
The likes I've never seen.

April promised rainbows
And blue skies overhead.
She promised perfumed breezes
And roses ruby red.

April promised springtime
In all her majesty,
And I wasn't disappointed
For she gave these gifts to me.

Nora M. Bozeman

My Friend

Thank you… for bringing sunshine
To my gray and gloomy days,
For being there when needed,
And for your caring, loving ways.

Thank you… for encouragement
When I was weary and distraught,
For words of consolation,
And for all the joy you brought.

Thank you… for all your prayers
That were made in my behalf,
For helping to erase my tears
And to replace them with a laugh.

I can face each new tomorrow,
For I know I can depend…
On God… who sent an angel,
And it is you… my precious friend.

Patience Allison Hartbauer

*When cares increase within me,
Your comfort gives me joy.
Psalm 94:19*

Without a Doubt

When the last snowflake has melted
Along the hill and way
And the sky's a brighter blue
Than it was yesterday.
When swollen buds on tree and bush
Are waiting for rebirth
And Mother Nature is intent
On washing clean the earth.

When pussy willow in the woods
Shows furry little toes
And the happy brooklet babbles,
Free of ice and snow.
When you see a crocus blooming
And your heart can't help but sing
Then you know without a doubt –
It's the coming of the Spring.

Kay Hoffman

The Creative Hand of God

I walked in the garden at even
Along the blossomy trail;
I saw the blooms in their beauty,
Some massive and some quite frail.

I watched as a flower unfolded,
I saw well-spent blossoms fall;
I smelled the sweet honeysuckle
That covered the garden wall.

I walked in the garden at even,
And there at that fragrant spot,
I saw in each flower of beauty
The creative hand of God.

Loise Pinkerton Fritz

*All things were made by Him;
and without Him was not any
thing made that was made.*
John 1:3

I Thank Thee, Lord

I thank Thee, Lord, for sunshine bright,
For peace and restful sleep at night,
For rosy dawns and birdsong trills,
For lacy trees and greening hills.

For beauty everywhere I look,
From mountains tall to shady nook,
From country lanes to emerald seas,
I thank Thee, Lord, for all of these.

I thank Thee, Lord, for friends so dear,
For all their warmth and love and cheer,
For home and health and family,
For daily gifts bestowed on me.

For music, poetry I love
That turn my thoughts to Thee above,
For special joys that bless my life,
And for Thy help in time of strife.

I thank Thee, Lord, I'm in Thy care,
For quiet times I spend in prayer,
For Thy unfailing love for me,
Thy promised hope… eternity!

        Beverly J. Anderson

A Morning Prayer

Today, Lord, give me courage,
If indeed it is Your will,
To stand for all things righteous,
All Your desires fulfill.

In my weakness I may falter,
Extend Your hand, I pray.
I cannot walk alone, dear Lord,
Please guide my path today.

May I portray Your goodness,
So those I meet may see
The wonder of Your power
As Your love shines through me.

And at the ending of this day,
I will thankfully behold
How You and I together, Lord,
Achieved a worthy goal.

Nancy W. Tant

A Few of My Favorite Things

Rainbows and butterflies
And a bluebird taking flight;
Fireflies and star-filled skies
And a full moon's shining light.

Oak trees tall, a whippoorwill's call,
Red roses drenched with dew;
Summer days where sunshine plays
And a misty mountain view.

A country lane, a sweet refrain,
A church's chiming bell –
Even when they're out of sight,
They hold me in their spell.

Nora M. Bozeman

*Charm and beauty delight
the eye, but better than
either, the flowers of the field.
Sirach 40:22*

Learn to Wait

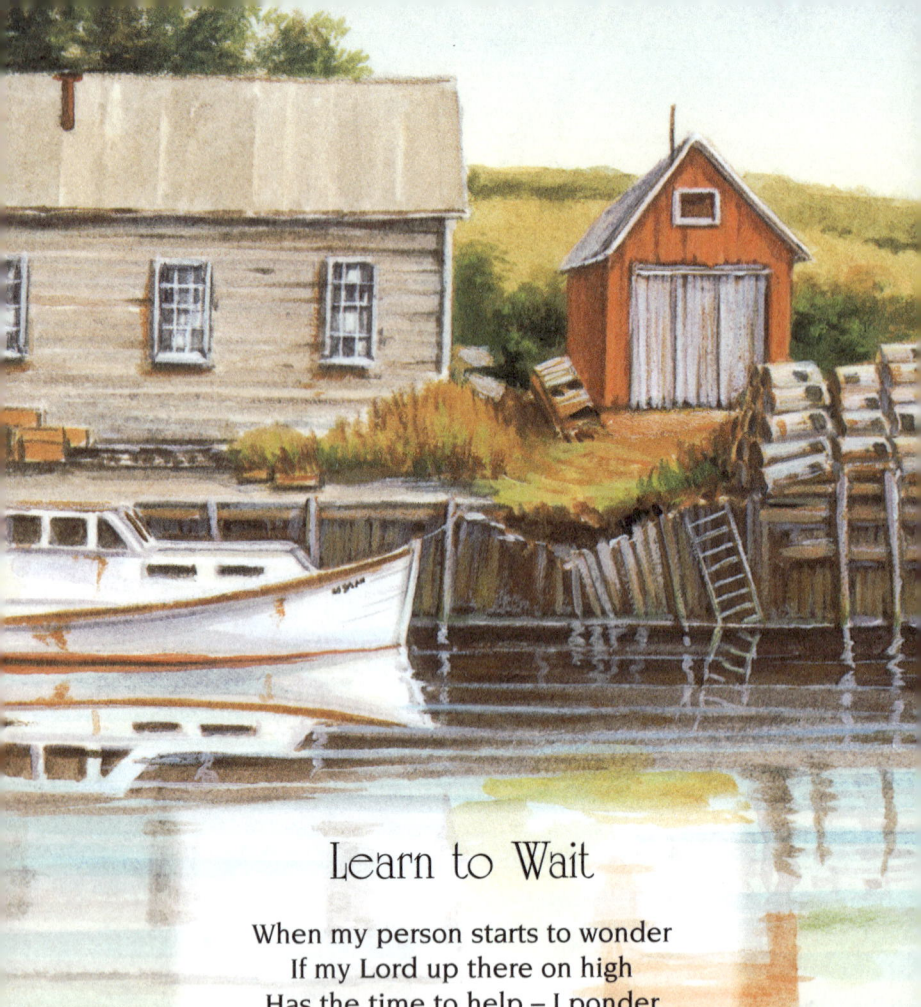

When my person starts to wonder
If my Lord up there on high
Has the time to help – I ponder
On my troubles and I sigh.

And my spirit is discouraged
With the burdens of the day,
And with each and every moment,
Feels more discouraged and dismayed.

Then I feel a gentle urging
To read His word anew,
For He's always there to listen
To my burdens and adieus.

It's my Savior, my Lord Jesus,
Who will listen to my woes,
And His word gives new assurance
That He cares for us below.

For He ne'er permits a burden
That He hasn't vowed to share.
It is we with such impatience
Who want immediate answers to our prayers.

Mildred Friend Roger Thomas

With His Love

With the love and grace of Jesus,
Every day we spend on earth
Will be time of joy and blessings –
Like our miracle of birth.
And we will forever prosper
In His love and holy care,
If we heed His warning wisdoms
That we find in Bible prayer.

With His blessings and His graces –
That He gives away with love –
We are sure of earthly comforts
And salvation, up above,
But we must be kind and Christian –
In the life we live each day –
To be worthy and deserving
Of the love He gives away.

Michael Dubina

Rise and Look Ahead

Dry your tears, look up and see –
It's another brand-new day.
Close that page in your book of life,
There's more to do and say.

The sun will shine on you again,
The clouds will roll away,
Flowers will bloom, birds will sing –
There'll be a brand-new day.

Don't be despondent
And of the future dread;
There's more of life still left for you…
Rise up and look ahead.

Ruth Moyer Gilmour

*The Lord has heard my prayer;
the Lord takes up my plea.*
Psalm 6:10

The Changing of the Guard

The hollyhocks have gone to seed
Like raisins in the sun.
The hummingbirds have flown away,
Their journey has begun.

It seems the days are shorter now;
A chill is in the air,
For soon the oak and maple
Will have new coats to wear.

In their coats of many colors,
The woods will be aglow
And the graying skies above us
Have promised early snow.

There are great expectations –
Parades with fife and drum,
In the spirit of Thanksgiving
And of holidays to come.

There's something about this moment
To energize the bard
As Nature marches forward
With the changing of the guard.

Clay Harrison

Enter Autumn

There are hillsides of gold
As Autumn unfolds,
Hillsides of gold and red.

There are pumpkins, bright orange,
And hay-laden barns,
Bittersweet by the shed.

In fields corn shocks stand
Across Autumn land,
Blue are the skies o'erhead.

By the stream sumac grows,
The leaves now red show,
Leaves that will soon be shed.

There are orchards ablaze
With apples, red-faced,
Fruit for the days ahead.

There are all these and more
To thank the Lord for
As Summer is put to bed.

Loise Pinkerton Fritz

Autumn Really Shines

Of each season that exists,
Autumn really shines;
Her colors are magnificent –
A touch from the Divine.

From flaming red oaks
To golden maple trees,
Only God could create
The beauty of the leaves!

Goldenrod and sumac
Spread across each field;
Oh, the blessings that erupt
From the bounty of her yield!

Decked with rows of orange pumpkins –
Soon a yummy pie or two,
Autumn shines in many ways
For she just loves to woo.

Reach out for her treasures
While they glitter so,
Then when Winter slowly slithers in,
Autumn memories with warmth will flow!

Linda C. Grazulis

Autumn in My Heart

Oh, Autumn, I would keep you
And never let you part,
But God has made the seasons,
So I must keep you in my heart.

The green of Summer is over
And it seems rather strange
That you slipped in so quietly
And set the earth aflame.

The beauty of the scarlet leaves
And those of rust and gold
Is a little of the magic
That the autumntime unfolds.

The woods are still and silent;
You can hear the dry leaves fall
While sitting on a hollow log
Under flaming trees quite tall.

Each season has a purpose
With memories sure to last,
But the wonder of the autumntime
Must leave us all too fast.

Shirley Hile Powell

Autumn Is a Gypsy Season

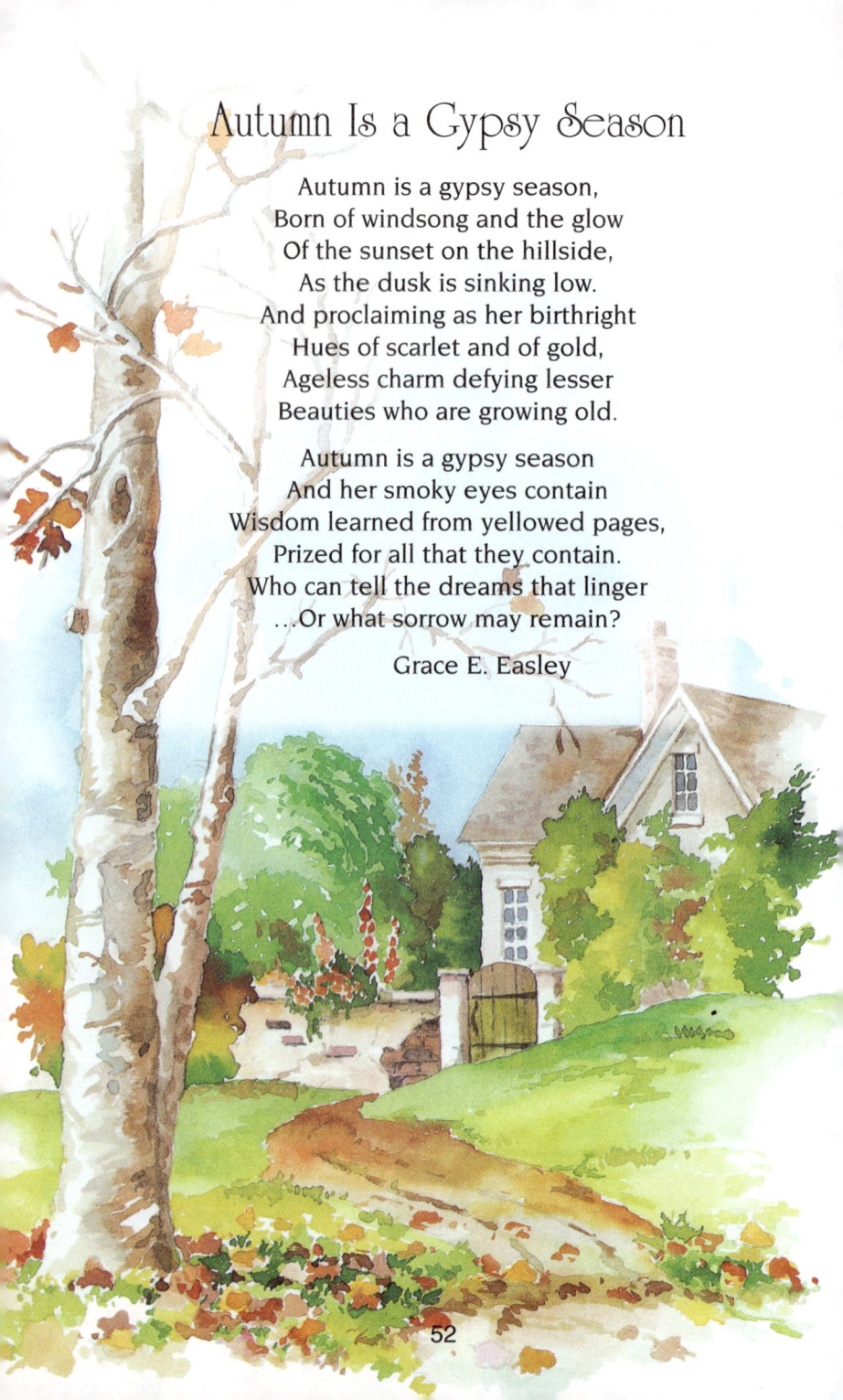

Autumn is a gypsy season,
Born of windsong and the glow
Of the sunset on the hillside,
As the dusk is sinking low.
And proclaiming as her birthright
Hues of scarlet and of gold,
Ageless charm defying lesser
Beauties who are growing old.

Autumn is a gypsy season
And her smoky eyes contain
Wisdom learned from yellowed pages,
Prized for all that they contain.
Who can tell the dreams that linger
…Or what sorrow may remain?

Grace E. Easley

Autumn's Aria

Autumn, dressed in glory,
Sings an operatic air
As pictures from earth's storybook
Are painted everywhere.

Bright forests, straddling valleys,
Draw their magic to the eye
While rolling inland rivers
Chant high praises to the sky.

Ground winds sweeping through the land
Reveal a treasure trove
Of brown-toned, red, and golden notes
Bespeaking God's great love.

For Winter's wondrous, great prelude
My heart is filled with gratitude.

Frankie Davis Oviatt

*Give to the Lord the glory due
God's name. Bow down before
the Lord's holy splendor!*
Psalm 29:2

Hold Fast to Your Mem'ries

Hold fast to your mem'ries –
Don't let them fade,
Ponder them daily
As new ones are made.

Keep them as fresh
As morningtime dew;
If you do them this favor,
They'll return it to you…

And come readily to mind
At your beck and call,
Let you defy time, and
Go back over the "wall…"

To the time and the place
Your heart holds most dear,
And the voice that you miss,
Once more you will hear.

The warm Summer air,
So fragrant with flowers,
Will caress you again
And drain away hours.

The feelings you knew
Will return in a rush
As you revel in mem'ry's
Soft, gentle hush.

Then, returning to tasks
Of this present day,
Somehow you're refreshed
As you go on your way.

Oh, hold on to your mem'ries!
Don't let them fade!
Ponder them daily
As new ones are made.

          Denise A. DeWald

Guiding Faith

Sometimes, dear Lord, when I'm perplexed
And troubles seem mountain-high,
I go to You in prayer for help
Then tackle them with a sigh.

There are no problems too large or small
That we can't solve together,
As long as the faith within my heart
Unites me with You forever.

Yesterday's worries have come and gone,
Today's will work out fine.
Tomorrow's we'll conquer together, Lord,
In Your own way and time.

Faith is truly a wonderful gift
And I thank my God each day,
For giving me the faith I have
To guide me along life's way.

Shirley Hile Powell

God Guides My Path

God's care and wisdom guides my path
Along life's broad highway,
And if I follow where He leads,
He'll help me not to stray.

And when life's paths may twist and turn,
I hold tight to His hand.
If through dim valleys I must tread
And I can't understand…

I have assurance God knows best,
And so I will not fear.
I'll trust His love and care for me
And know that He is near.

I'm glad God's wisdom guides my path;
He planned each step I take.
In faith I follow for I know
He maketh no mistake.

Beverly J. Anderson

May God's Love Abide Within You

May God's love abide within you
And fill you with His light
So you will not fear the darkness
On a never-ending night.

May His love always sustain you
And give you strength to try
When the world has turned against you
And you think you could cry.

May His love become your lighthouse
When the storms of life assail
And the arms of faith uphold you
As you ride out the gale.

God's love is everlasting
And free to one and all.
It's the power that sustains you
If ever you should fall.

May you never fear the darkness
Or the creatures of the night.
May God's love abide within you
And be your guiding light.

Clay Harrison

Prayer Power

Don't vaguely wonder
When you pray
If God can hear
The words you say.
His listening ear
Is close to you.
His caring love
Surrounds you, too.

It's you who needs
To tune your ear,
Your heart and soul
To better hear
God's timely answer...
Then you'll find
Through Him new goals
And peace of mind.

Amy C. Ellis

Blessed Friend

You have a beauty rare
And a soul that is aglow;
I feel I've been so blest
For such a friend to know.

You laugh with me often
And cry with me, too.
Such empathy for a friend,
I know your heart is true.

Many blessings to you, dear friend,
And I hope that God will see
All of your days filled with joy
To be as happy as you've made me.

Susie Hutton

*The grace of the Lord
Jesus be with you.*
1 Corinthians 16:23

Splendor and majesty go before Him; praise and joy are in His holy place.
1 Chronicles 16:27

Beauty and Splendor

There is beauty and splendor
In the dawn of the morn
When on yonder's horizon,
A new day is born.

There is beauty and splendor
In the quiet of the day,
In the sweet solitude
When I'm kneeling to pray.

There is beauty and splendor
In the darkness of night,
When God's presence I feel
And the stars shining bright.

There is beauty and splendor
In a sweet lullaby,
Sung soft by a mother
To hush baby's cry.

Katherine Smith Matheney

It's Spring Again!

When sleepy crocuses lift their heads
And robins reappear,
When dandelions sprout everywhere,
We know at last Spring's here!
The grass is greening and the scent
Of budding roses fills
The air with fragrant, sweet perfume,
As golden daffodils
Turn one by one toward the sun
And bask in sparkling light,
While all about signs of rebirth
Reveal a future bright
With promise of great things to come
If we but trust and pray
To God for guidance and His love
Each night and each new day.

Vi B. Chevalier

In Silence

It is not things that make you happy,
But the silent things of day;
You cannot hear the blessings
Nor the prayers that come your way.

You cannot hear the smiles
When someone thinks of you
Or when they're feeling lonesome
Or when their hearts are blue.

You cannot hear the longing
When you are far away
Or the lonesomeness you're feeling
At the end of each new day.

You cannot hear His message,
His face or golden smile,
But you know that He is with you
In silence, all the while.

James Joseph Huesgen

*The Lord look upon you kindly
and give you peace!*
Numbers 6:26

Home

A castle to so many,
A refuge for the rest,
Tho traveling does excite me,
It's home I love the best.

The good times have been many,
Yet it is plain to see,
Both sad and happy times I've had
Have made my memories.

The walls have rung with laughter
And tears were sometimes shed,
But through it all I've managed
To always look ahead…

To thank Him for His blessings
And always put Him first;
He feeds my soul with happiness
And quenches every thirst.

When my travels on this earth are done,
There's a place I want to go,
Be it cabin or palatial manse,
It's home… the sweetest word I know.

   Shirley Takacs

Be my rock and refuge, my secure stronghold;
for You are my rock and fortress.
Psalm 71:3

Summer's Umbrella

The umbrella of Summer's
A picturesque one;
It's a heavenly blue
With a sunshiny sun.

To this showy umbrella
Are added the birds
With colorful plumage
Too brilliant for words.

Its beauty increases
With bright butterflies,
Small playful bunnies
And high-flying kites.

The umbrella of Summer
Is stitched with these scenes
And tucked with bright flowers
On borders and seams.

Loise Pinkerton Fritz

Butterflies

I marvel in the artistry
That made the butterflies I see
And gave them beauty, life and form –
And hues of rainbows, dusk and dawn.
I'm sure that only God could weave
Such holy art with majesty
And give it wings with which to fly
And bless with beauty, earth and sky.

Michael Dubina

*The Lord hath made all
things for His own ends…*
Proverbs 16:4

A Greater God

A child sees God with his little mind,
And cannot perceive His magnitude,
But as he grows in wisdom and stature,
A different picture of God ensues.

Like a blindfold as it falls away,
He sees an ever-widening view;
And as his world becomes much larger,
His God becomes much larger, too.

The small problems he knew as a child
Become problems of a different kind;
Soon he falls upon his knees to God,
As a man who's left childhood behind.

Although he now prays as a man,
He must still retain that childlike heart.
Though sweet innocence has flown away,
He sings louder now, "How Great Thou Art."

It seems aging changes many things
As through this life our footsteps trod.
When we remember the God of our youth –
He's perceived as an even greater God!

Barbara Cagle Ray

*...great and wonderful are all
Your works, Lord God Almighty.
Revelation 15:3*

As God Gives

As God gives drink to the flowers,
So may He water you;
May His living waters satisfy,
Overflow as sweet morning dew!

And like the sun gives its sunrays,
Causing flowers to softly unfold –
May the Father's love surrounding you
Open blessings as yet untold!

Lynn Fenimore Nuzzi

More Than the Sun

His sun comes up in scarlet skies,
Goes westward willingly;
His rains are soft upon my fields
And He is good to me.

He blesses me with plenty's face;
My barns all overflow;
My fertile fields await His Spring
When I shall plow each row…

In symmetry – like watered silk –
In ribbons brown and rich.
I'll thank this God who sees to me,
Who gives me knowledge which…

Creates the braids of woven green
Against horizons blue;
This God I trust more than the sun –
To praise Him is my due.

Henry W. Gurley

*Yours the day and Yours
the night; You set the
moon and sun in place.*
Psalm 74:16

Aftermath

September is so beautiful,
And yet a little sad –
It spells the end of Summer
And the heavenly days we've had.

Swimming at the ocean beach,
Picnics in the park,
And chatting on our porches
For hours after dark!

Sitting 'long the riverbank
To hear gazebo bands,
The drives into the country
For visiting farmer stands.

How pleasant are the Summer days,
Bright with sun and flowers.
The wonderful scent of rain
In softly cooling showers.

Though I love you dearly, Summer…
I welcome now September –
A lovely aftermath
Of a Summer to remember!

Janice Taylor Wright

God Has Shown the Way

I have learned to love from Jesus
Like a baby learns to talk;
He has shown the way for me in life,
The path that I should walk.
Sometimes we fail to listen,
But He will lead you by the hand;
In your darkest moments,
He will help you understand.

He is there when you are yearning,
He hears your call each day;
When you're lost upon the path of life,
He is there to show the way.
At times in our quest for righteousness
There are times when we may fall;
He will be there to catch you
For He's our Savior, after all.

James Joseph Huesgen

Summer Glory

Poppies and roses grow by my door
With lilacs and zinnias in colors galore.

Bee balm and foxglove are growing there, too,
And every day I see something new.

Robins and bluebirds visit each day
While cardinals and martins frolic and play.

Hummingbirds sup at my feeder each day.
Their visits are brief, but sweet memories stay.

Sunflowers smile down from ten feet or more –
Bright visions of Vincent decades before.

Soft, Summer breezes waltz with the trees,
And rambling roses go where they please.

Each day brings a message fresh from the sod
That we have been blessed by a wonderful God!

Clay Harrison

Sermon on the Shore

Today I walked along the shore
As dawn began to break.
The stars began to fade away
As Heaven came awake.

The sky became a canopy
Of purple, mauve and blue,
And the clouds wore scarlet ribbons
Before the show was through.

Breakers hummed a melody
Upon the rocks below,
And seagulls sang a hymn of praise
With feathered robes aglow.

The sun ascended to its throne
Like a million times before,
And God blessed me once again
With a sermon on the shore.

Clay Harrison

Troubled Waters

Let Him walk upon the waters
Of all troubles, friend –
See Him calm the raging storm
And bring it to an end.

"Be not afraid," He whispers,
"I will calm your troubled sea –
Look not at the rolling waves,
Just look, dear one, at Me."

"I'll take your hand in Mine –
The fearful storm will pass,
I'll whisper, 'Peace, be still,'
And your sea will be as glass."

The troubled waters won't engulf –
He'll make the stormy winds a sigh,
Oh, sweet words of Christ –
"Fear not, for it is I!"

Ruth Martindale

Peace, Be Still

I pray that I shall not in blindness grope,
But see with vision unclouded and clear;
And know when to speak a word of hope,
 Or by my actions say, "I really care."

When the sea of life is tempest-tossed,
For a friend or foe, let me do Thy will –
And, like Jesus, calm a troubled soul,
As He calmed the waves with, "Peace, be still."

Barbara Cagle Ray

*The Lord look upon you kindly
and give you peace!*
Numbers 6:26

Autumn Magic

I found the Autumn magic
One bright October day,
In every splash of color
Among the leaves at play.
This lovely, changing season
Just at the Summer's end,
'Neath the skies of blue above –
A very special blend.

The Autumn shone so brightly
Along each country path,
And loaned a touch of nature –
A shining autograph.
She colored every hilltop,
Each Summer tree of green,
Then tossed the leaves in splendor
Atop each creek and stream.

God's world – a changing wonder –
As leaves piled thick and deep,
Beginning of the Autumn,
Each Summer day complete.
Before the cold of Winter,
Soft breezes still at play,
A touch of Autumn magic
To bless October's way.

Garnett Ann Schultz

*Give thanks to the Lord who is good,
whose love endures forever!*
Psalm 107:1

Interlude

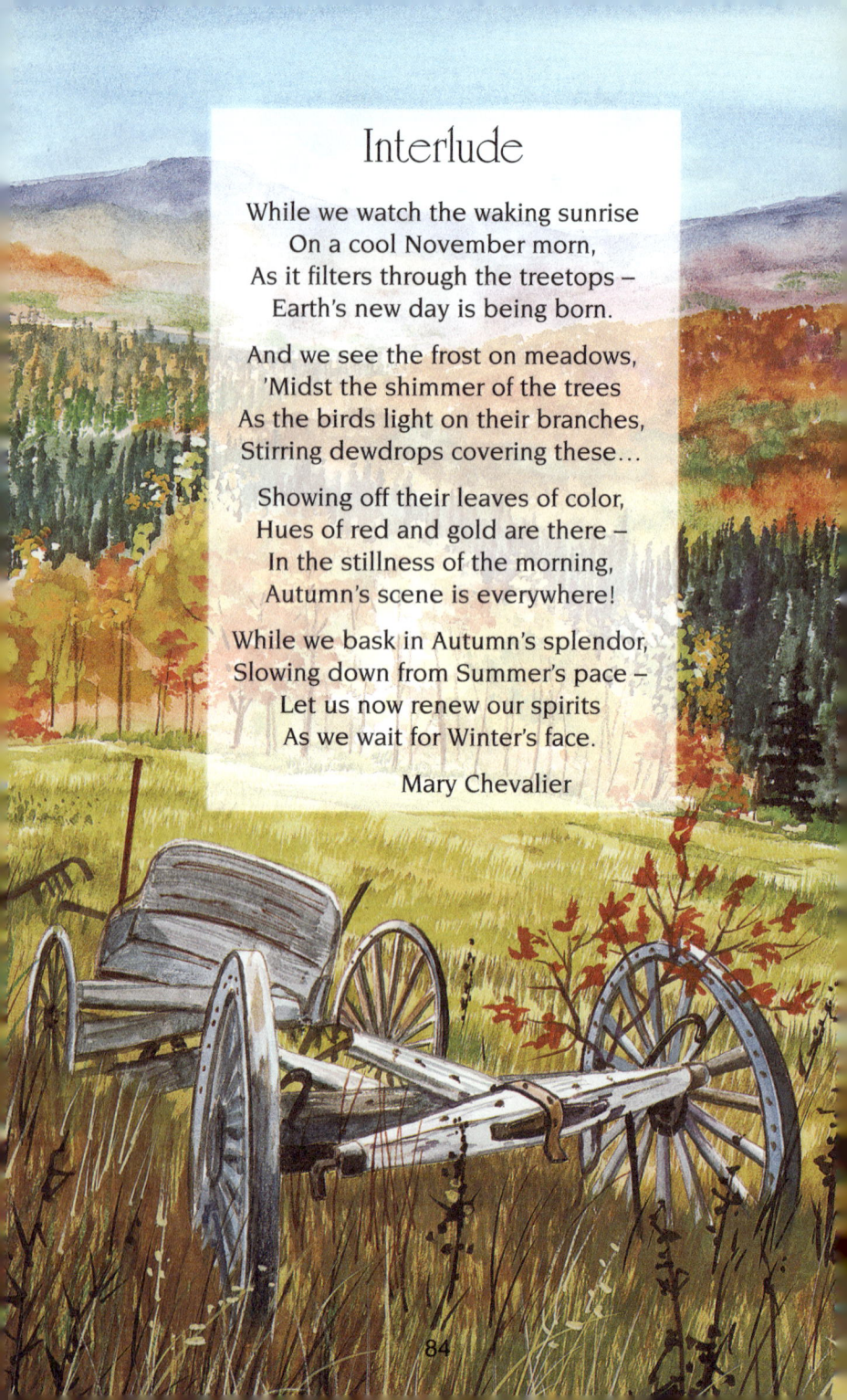

While we watch the waking sunrise
On a cool November morn,
As it filters through the treetops –
Earth's new day is being born.

And we see the frost on meadows,
'Midst the shimmer of the trees
As the birds light on their branches,
Stirring dewdrops covering these…

Showing off their leaves of color,
Hues of red and gold are there –
In the stillness of the morning,
Autumn's scene is everywhere!

While we bask in Autumn's splendor,
Slowing down from Summer's pace –
Let us now renew our spirits
As we wait for Winter's face.

Mary Chevalier

I Lose My Heart to Autumn

I lose my heart to Autumn,
It happens every year;
For Autumn is but a gypsy,
So full of warmth and cheer.

Dressed in dazzling red and gold,
Strolling o'er hill and way,
She flaunts her beauty unabashed
And draws all eyes her way.

The queen of every harvest ball,
By Mother Nature crowned;
A spendthrift at a county fair,
She flings her jewels around.

I know that Autumn's clever,
For her I'm easy prey;
She beckons with a warm, bright smile
And steals my heart away.

Kay Hoffman

*It is the Lord's blessing that brings wealth,
and no effort can substitute for it.*
Proverbs 10:22

The Right Road

There are many routes to follow
In the atlas of our days.
Some are straight and steady
And others, unmarked ways.

Some pathways lead to sorrow
With ambitions unfulfilled.
Some roads have tricky detours
Life's choices help to build.

But if we read the signposts
When roadblocks make us stop,
With the map of faith to guide us,
We can reach the mountaintop.

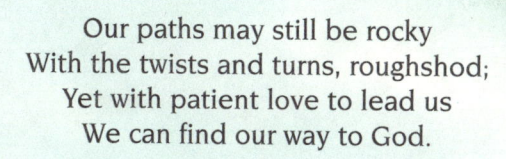

Our paths may still be rocky
With the twists and turns, roughshod;
Yet with patient love to lead us
We can find our way to God.

Then, basking in His sunshine,
Weary now and sore of limb,
We will know eternal glory
When, at last, we rest in Him.

Jean Conder Soule

Nature's Tapestries

There're no medieval tapestries
Whose beauty can compare
With an orange-leafed tree in Fall
Where hangs the pink-tinged pear.

There are no jewels in caches
Or hidden treasure troves
Quite as picturesque or colorful
As red-crowned trees in groves.

The warp and woof of Autumn
Weave patterns of gold threads –
Works in vivid colors,
Like bronze from aster beds.

The tapestries of Nature
Hang on sun-drenched days,
Reflecting Autumn's splendor
In all its vibrant rays.

Virginia Borman Grimmer

Where Did the Summer Go?

What happened to the Summer?
I really couldn't say.
I'm sure it must have taken wing
And quickly flown away.
Just yesterday was springtime,
A robin told me so.
Now could it be September's here?
Where did the Summer go?

What happened to that June night,
That sweet and happy thought,
The pleasant days of dreaming
That mid-July had brought?
Vacations long since over,
The Winter just ahead,
The Summer quickly fading
And Autumn glows instead.

What happened to the roses?
My goodness they look blue.
Their petals slowly falling,
Their leaves are dying, too.
What happened? I've the answer –
It isn't strange at all…
Old Mother Nature's Summer
Is changing into Fall.

Garnett Ann Schultz

Winter's Silence

The days are growing shorter,
The sun is turning red;
I must take my evening stroll
Before I go to bed.

I walk upon the icy lake,
And the only sound I hear
Is booming of the crackling ice,
Oh, so shiny, blue and clear.

Its beauty melts my weary heart
On this evening's rendezvous,
As laughter rings in the quiet night,
Life's joys I now review.

For hours I roam through fields of snow
While the silence sets the mood.
Here I can pray and meditate
In a peaceful interlude.

I do enjoy my family,
My work, my friends and such;
But on these silent Winter nights,
With God I keep in touch.

Angie Monnens

*May grace and peace be yours in
abundance through knowledge of God
and of Jesus our Lord.*
2 Peter 1:2

Winter's Snow

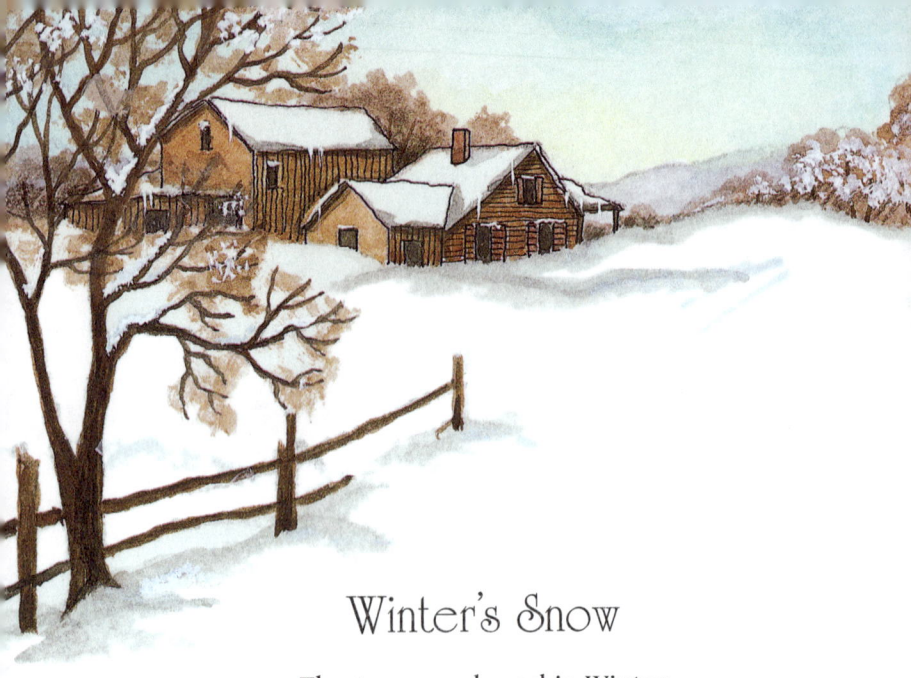

The trees are bared in Winter
As the leaves turn brown and die.
Tangled roots entwine on frozen ground
As sounds of wind give sigh.

God sends a gentle falling snow
That covers the barren ground.
The wonders that my eyes behold
Find God's beauty all around.

I'm thankful for the wintertime
That brings me untold pleasures
And for the days of silence,
Another of God's unique treasures.

The earth becomes a wonderland
As it glistens in the moonlight's glow.
God sends another masterpiece
With the pristine Winter snow.

Shirley Hile Powell

Winter's Magic

Of all Nature's seasons,
I love the Winter best –
It is a sleepy, quiet time,
The time for growth and rest.
It is when the trees are bare
That you can clearly see
A robin or a cardinal
Upon a maple tree.
It is when the river is frozen
And covered by the snow
That you can appreciate the life
That is swimming down below.
Those simple, quiet wonders
That only Winter brings –
Eggnog and candied apples,
Sleigh rides and skating rinks.
I know Autumn is brighter,
Summer is warmer than the rest,
I like the gentle kiss of Spring,
But I love Winter best.

Elizabeth Lyulkin

Climb Your Mountain

There are many mountains in this life,
Some impassable it seems,
Like the ones which rise within us
That overshadow hopes and dreams.
Each mountain has a passageway
With its rough and rocky trail,
Ever treacherously upward
Where fears are soon unveiled.

Let perseverance be your guide
For it's all you truly need
To climb your way to victory –
Don't give up, you will succeed.
The rocks are merely obstacles
To discourage and defeat
And no mountain is impossible,
Every mountain can be beat.
If you'll endure, I'm very sure
You'll ride the wind on high,
Like an eagle on the mountaintop,
Wings outstretched and perched to fly.

        Gina Mazzullo Laurin

Memories

Across the pages of a life
Unwritten stories form themselves,
And each is kept in some strange way
Within the memory's vast bookshelves.

And often new events recall
With striking suddenness, once more,
The long forgotten happenings
Of early years that went before.

So we are blessed by memories
Through all our days since childhood,
By lessons learned and joys relived
With those who loved and understood!

John C. Bonser

There Is Time

There's always time in every life
To live a better way,
To be more giving of ourselves
And take more time to pray;
There's always time to try anew
What we have failed to do
That would do honor to the Lord
And win His blessings, too.

But we get tired and worn by time
And hurts and trials of life –
And shattered dreams of love and hope
Add heartaches to our strife.
Yet, there is still the room and time
To live a better way
If we will only love and care –
Like in our yesterdays.

Michael Dubina

Springtime's Grand Design

Springtime wore a day designed
In apple blossom grace.
Sunbeams greeted her with glee
And gently kissed her face.

Springtime wore a gown of green
And a sky of sapphire blue.
She waltzed across the misty morn
And sprinkled diamond-dew.

Springtime wore a balmy breeze
And bathed in pale moonlight.
She danced among the daffodils
On a lilac-scented night.

Springtime wore a rose bouquet
And flowers so sublime.
Her treasures bright and beautiful
Are springtime's grand design.

Nora M. Bozeman

Springtime

Springtime is a special time
To share God's wondrous love,
To thank Him for each blessing
That He sends from Heaven above.

He gives us so much beauty
In showing us He cares,
And springtime seems so special,
We can see Him everywhere.

With sunshine from the heavens
And flowers reaching t'ward the sky,
We can feel His presence near us
As the clouds go floating by.

As the raindrops fall upon us,
We can feel His special touch,
It seems that He is saying,
"I love you very much."

Yes, springtime seems so special
With God's presence everywhere.
He covers each and every thing
To show us that He cares.

Bonnie Knapp

Together

Whenever we're together,
There's a certain atmosphere
Of rosy colored hours
That miraculously appear.
I cannot quite describe it,
But the moment you are near,
I see a colored rainbow,
And the clouds all disappear.

Whenever we're together,
There is sweetness, there is light,
And tensions seem to vanish,
And the sharing seems so right.
And no harsh words are spoken,
For the lips of love are kind,
And my heart is full of wonder
At the beauty that I find.

Whenever we're together,
There is no foolish pride,
Only understanding that
Can shut the world outside.
It may be we are more alike
Than anyone can guess,
Whose deepest needs are answered
In each other's happiness.

          Grace E. Easley

Early Spring

Hazy, misty, springtime morning,
With a coolness in the air –
Hosts of chirping, restless songbirds
Spread their wings with ardent flair!

Each, it seems, excels the other
With its own impressive tune –
Calling out in lofty splendor
As they perch midst redbud's bloom!

Only God in all His glory
Could create this wondrous scene;
Let us pause, inhale its beauty,
Meditate – and lessons glean!

Mary Chevalier

Renewal

Spring brings with it a renewal
Of the faith God's children share.
I look around and hope abounds,
As blossoms burst forth everywhere.

Each tree is turning leafy green;
Sit beneath its boughs and see –
You'll feel as though you're sharing
God's wondrous love and hospitality!

The songbirds make my heart rejoice,
And fragrant flowers feed my soul.
Bulbs push forth from frozen earth
And transform to daffodils of gold!

Spring was made for weary souls;
Just one more blessing God does send –
For all things bright and beautiful
Seem to renew man's faith again.

Barbara Cagle Ray

*They that hope in the Lord will renew their
strength, they will soar as with eagles' wings;
they will run and not grow weary,
walk and not grow faint.*
Isaiah 40:31

Safe in His Arms

I built a fence around my heart,
Invincible and tall.
I wanted no one near or far
To scale that sturdy wall.

For years this fortress kept me safe
Inside my barricade.
Then suddenly, I heard a voice,
Which left me quite dismayed.

Who dared to come and call my name
And linger at my gate?
Should I go and seek him out
Or let him stand and wait?

Then beside my wall I saw
A Stranger waiting there.
He spoke my name again with love
And understanding care.

This Friend had come to live with me
And share each lonely day.
My wall no longer shut Him out;
I knew He'd come to stay.

So then I cast aside the bars
That kept my life apart
And welcomed my dear Savior in
To live within my heart!

Jean Conder Soule

Summertime Sunday

When church bells on Sunday morning
Fill the air with hymns of praise,
Summer flowers add their beauty
To God's bright and joyous days.

More than ever we remember,
With a warm and grateful prayer,
God sends life's hope and harmony
And His wondrous blessings beyond compare.

Elisabeth Weaver Winstead

*The just will rejoice and take refuge in the
Lord; all the upright will glory in their God.
Psalm 64:11*

Farewell, Green Fields

Farewell, green fields of Summer,
The splendor of the grass,
Flecked with colors dancing
Along remote, untrodden paths.

Farewell, wild crimson roses,
Deflowered by the wind,
Lush petals crowned with glory
Now turning pale and specter-thin.

Farewell, my rustic countryside,
Tranquil haven of repose,
Until the fields are emerald green
And the bloom is on the rose.

Barbara Cagle Ray

*Return, O my soul, to your tranquility,
for the Lord has been good to you.*
Psalm 116:7

Life's Road

I walk the path down life's rutted road
And look on every side.
There's beauty in each fallen leaf
According to my guide.

Some trees are old and scarred with marks
Cut deep into the bark,
While others are just starting out –
Young and tender in their hearts.

I watch the water rushing by
Underneath the bridge,
Carrying all the sticks and stones
Cast down from yonder ridge.

Birds and animals feast from the land,
The flowers smell so good.
There's the hint of rain in the evening air
And the wisp of smoke from burning wood.

I have no need to own possessions
While waiting for the Master's call.
All I need is what He's given –
Just look around! I have it all.

Elaine Fowser

Let your eyes look straight ahead and your glance be directly forward. Survey the path for your feet, and let all your ways be sure.
Proverbs 4:25-26

Winds

No music holds more grandeur,
Nor more wondrous, perfect worth,
Than the myriad tones and voices
Of the winds that sweep the earth.
From the gentle, whispered sighing
Of a fragrant Summer breeze
To the wild and strident crying
Of a gale o'er Winter seas.

Minnie Boyd Popish

Knee-Deep in Beauty

Give me a field full of daisies,
And the wild birds singing their song;
On a June day that's knee-deep in beauty,
Praise God! This is where I belong!

Let me breathe in the scent of warm pine trees
While bright butterflies weave in and out,
And thank God for my place in creation,
For this is what life's all about.

Lola Neff Merritt

One thing I ask of the Lord; this I seek: To dwell in the Lord's house all the days of my life, to gaze on the Lord's beauty, to visit His temple.
Psalm 27:4

The Narrow Path

Lord, guide me down the narrow path,
The one that leads to Thee.
Reach down and hold my hand, I pray,
For I know that You love me.

Without Your love, I could not bear
To cope with daily strife.
If not for You, I could not live
A truly Christian life.

How great Your love for sinful me;
How much You still must bear.
Lord, keep me on the righteous path
And see that I remain there.

My flesh is weak and my will is free,
But if I take a firm stand
To try and walk the narrow path,
My life will be Yours to command.

Never leave me alone, dear Lord,
Be forever at my side.
Please make Your home in my poor heart,
Where Your peace and love abide.

Shirley Hile Powell

September Days

September days are in between
The Summer's gold – the Autumn scene,
Last moments sweet of flowers in bloom
And high above a harvest moon.
The birds still sing so happily
Within the magic maple tree.

September lends her tranquil charms
And tucks the Summer in her arms.
So soon the Autumn days will smile
And dress the trees in gorgeous style.
The colors bright we hold so dear
When Autumn comes to bless us here.

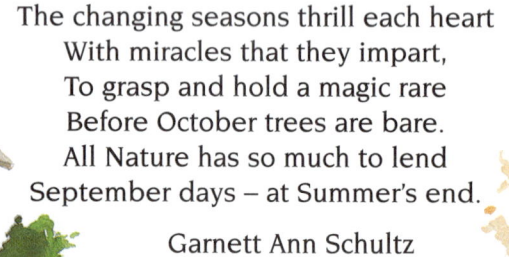

The changing seasons thrill each heart
With miracles that they impart,
To grasp and hold a magic rare
Before October trees are bare.
All Nature has so much to lend
September days – at Summer's end.

Garnett Ann Schultz

Autumn Winds

The winds of Spring were full of song;
I ran too fast to hear.
Now I find the music gone
As Winter clouds draw near.

Summer's blooms have faded,
Their fragrance lingers on.
Flowers of the heart
Are never truly gone.

The leaves have turned to amber,
Twilight brings a chill.
Shadows stretch dark fingers,
Autumn winds grow still.

There is time to sow and time to grow;
The seasons make their claim.
Winter winds are blowing…
God just called my name.

C. David Hay

*All you winds, bless the Lord; praise
and exalt Him above all forever.*
Daniel 3:65

Old Country Church Beside the Road

I saw the old church standing there
As I walked on a tranquil country road,
Underneath the boughs of an old oak tree,
Displaying its leaves of red and gold.

It was very old and worn with time;
The paint was faded and growing thin.
It had a rusty, crosslike spire;
I felt compelled to wander in.

A rusty gate creaked open wide,
The path of stones was bathed in shade.
A sign hung just above the door:
"Welcome all whom God hath made."

I could almost hear "Amazing Grace,"
As in solemn stillness I did rest.
Squirrels scurried across oaken beams
And birds were chirping in their nests.

Of all the loveliness I've seen
On God's great earth, that I recall,
The most priceless things to me are those
That cost me not a cent at all!

I walked outside the old church door
And turned to steal a look behind.
It was then I smiled and realized
The truthfulness of that old church sign:

"Welcome all whom God hath made,"
Most certainly that day rang true.
Those furry creatures housed inside
Must know that God hath made them, too!

Barbara Cagle Ray

*Welcome one another, then, as Christ
welcomed you, for the glory of God.*
Romans 15:7

I Love My Little Home, Dear Lord

I love my little home, dear Lord,
Oh yes, I do indeed,
And since Thou art the head of it,
I have no want or need.
Thy gifts are far too numerous,
Thou givest daily bread,
Thy watch Thou keepeth as I sleep
In my warm, cozy bed.
And while I do the dishes, Lord,
I talk to Thee in prayer,
Thus give to You my burdens all,
Each heartache and each care.
And whene'er my soul is thirsting,
I give to You my cup,
All too soon it's overflowing,
With joy You fill it up.
I'm grateful for the sunshine, too,
And rainbows in the sky,
For moonbeams and twinkling stars
And clouds all drifting by.
I'm grateful for so many things,
How could I e'er repay
For all that You have done for me,
The gifts You send each day?

Mary E. Herrington

God Gives the Full-Ear Yield

The corn is waving in the fields
Throughout the countryside;
The amber tips sway in the breeze,
The ears will soon be ripe.

The blessed joys of harvesttime
Lie wrapped within these fields;
Man sows at seedtime kernels small;
God gives the full-ear yield.

Loise Pinkerton Fritz

Then God said, "Let the earth bring forth vegetation: every kind of plant that bears fruit with its seed in it." And so it happened.
Genesis 1:11

An Autumntime Melody

I often think of autumntime
As a lovely melody,
From the hooting of a barn owl
To the swishing of the leaves.

The chirping of cicadas
Adds a special kind of tune,
Reminding me to relish Fall
For Winter's arriving very soon.

In a V-formation heading south
Geese are squawking up a storm,
But in a nearby farmer's garden
Orange pumpkins are silently being born.

A whispering wind rustles
Fields now ripened with sumac and goldenrod,
Colorful oaks and maples
Have their own way of proclaiming God.

So listen to the music
Of a sweet autumntime melody,
It will always be a classic
And sung each year so beautifully!

Linda C. Grazulis

Winter Jewel

See the shiny diamond
That sparkles in the sun?
I'm not sure of its carats,
Perhaps "One-million-one."
Its value is quite priceless,
But bound to plunge, I fear,
As other snowflakes fall to join
This first one of the year.

Bea Lotz

*Frost and chill, bless the Lord; praise
and exalt Him above all forever.*
Daniel 3:69

Come Winter

The lawn lays thick with apple leaves,
A crisp, north wind blows in;
The garden's cleared and empty,
The potatoes gathered in.

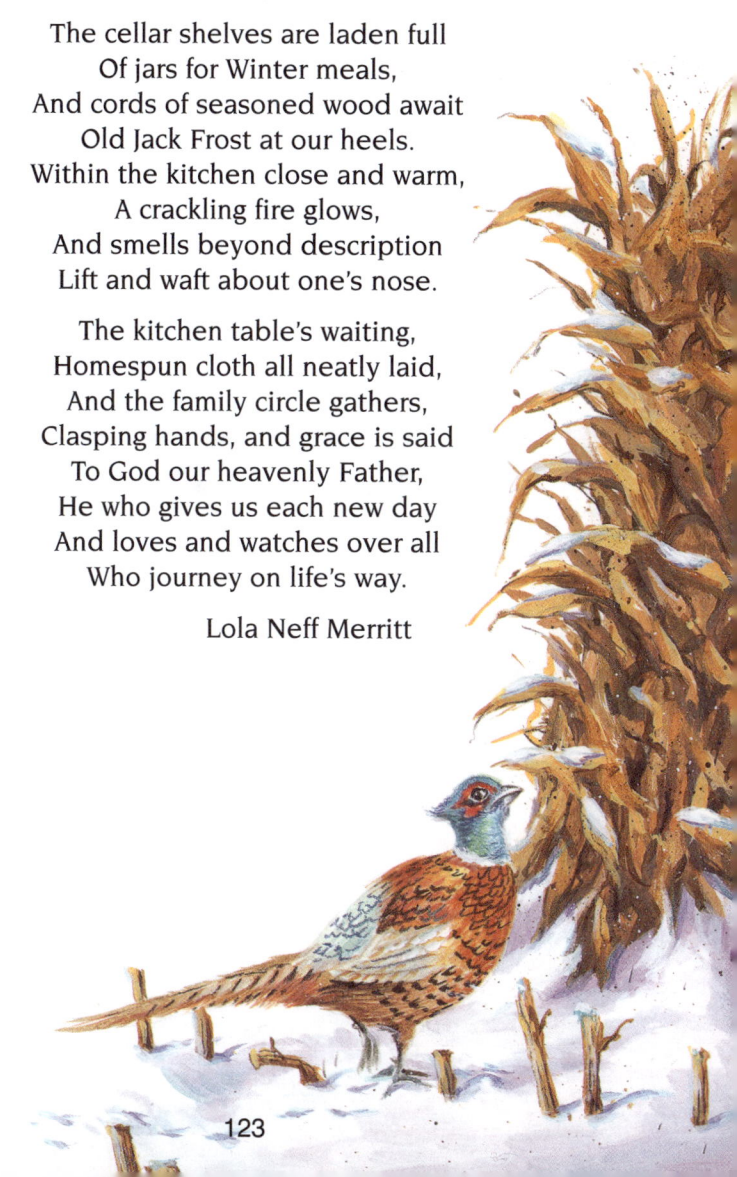

The cellar shelves are laden full
Of jars for Winter meals,
And cords of seasoned wood await
Old Jack Frost at our heels.
Within the kitchen close and warm,
A crackling fire glows,
And smells beyond description
Lift and waft about one's nose.

The kitchen table's waiting,
Homespun cloth all neatly laid,
And the family circle gathers,
Clasping hands, and grace is said
To God our heavenly Father,
He who gives us each new day
And loves and watches over all
Who journey on life's way.

Lola Neff Merritt

Earth's Dark Floor and Snowflakes

Whiteness veiled the village
As sparkling snowflakes fell;
Garbed in white were hillsides,
Forests, meadows, dells.

Winter's darkened earth-floor
Became a sparkling sight,
All because of snowflakes
God sent to earth that night.

What a transformation!
God changed the earth's darkened floor
Into one of whiteness
By opening Heaven's door.

Earth's dark floor and snowflakes…
Just then my mind was stirred;
I recalled God's promise,
According to His word.

Though our sins be scarlet,
They'll be made white as snow
If we'll trust in Jesus,
Redeemer of our souls.

Loise Pinkerton Fritz

*Come now, and let us reason together, saith
the Lord: Though your sins be as scarlet,
they shall be as white as snow…*
Isaiah 1:18

Treasure Beneath the Snow

The flower box outside my window,
Where petunias flourished in the Spring,
Is now heaped high with Winter white –
Such silent beauty did the night hours bring!

The most brilliant flash of fiery red
Has found my treasure beneath the snow.
I filled the box with seeds last night –
How did this exquisite redbird know?